Leeds
Travel Guide

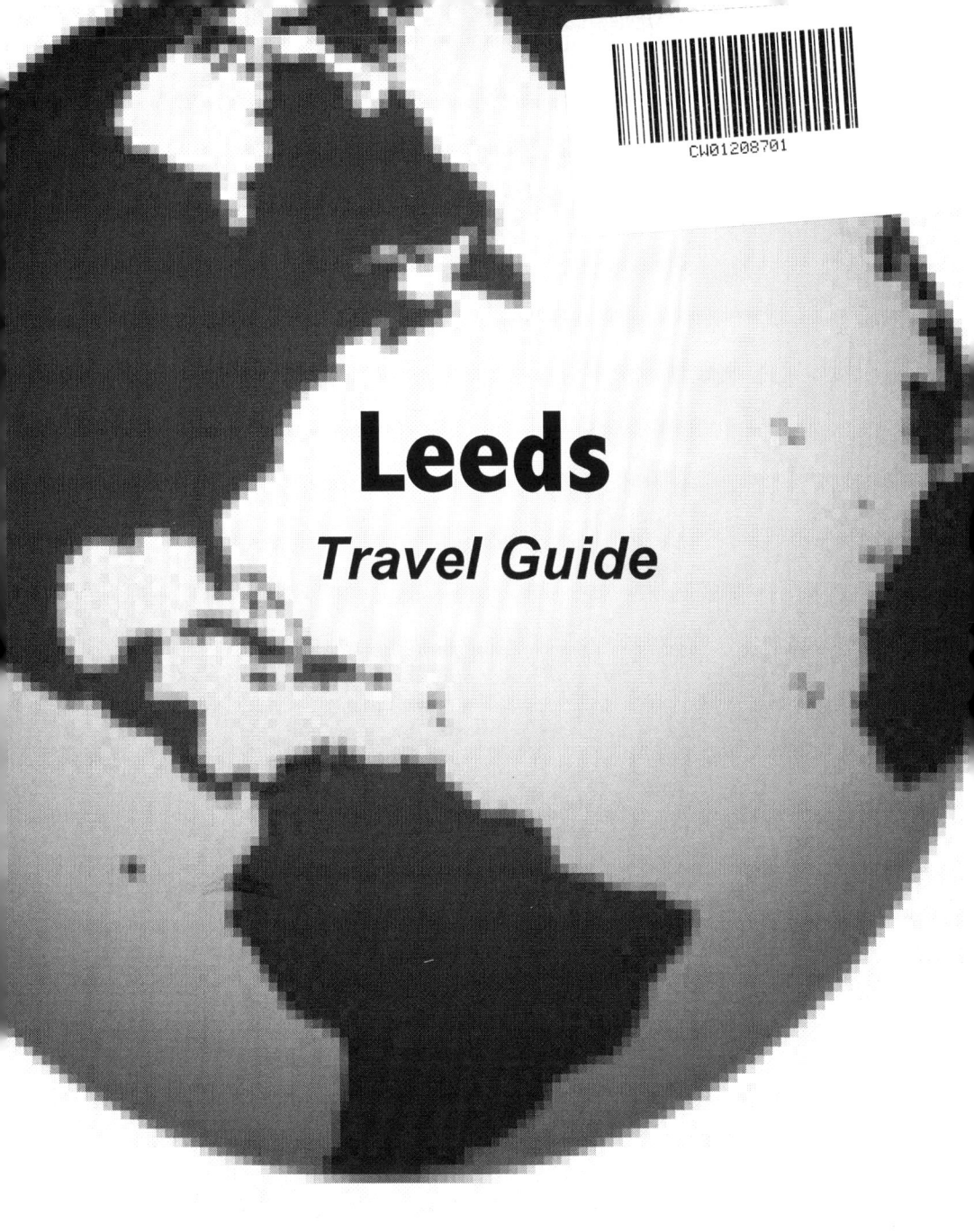

Quick Trips Series

No part of this publication may be reproduced, stored in a retrieval system, or transmitted, in any form or by any means without the prior written permission of the publisher, nor be otherwise circulated in any form of binding or cover other than that in which it is published and without similar condition being imposed on the subsequent purchaser. If there are any errors or omissions in copyright acknowledgements the publisher will be pleased to insert the appropriate acknowledgement in any subsequent printing of this publication. Although we have taken all reasonable care in researching this book we make no warranty about the accuracy or completeness of its content and disclaim all liability arising from its use.

Copyright © 2016, Astute Press
All Rights Reserved.

Table of Contents

LEEDS — 6
- 🌐 CUSTOMS & CULTURE 7
- 🌐 GEOGRAPHY 8
- 🌐 WEATHER & BEST TIME TO VISIT 11

SIGHTS & ACTIVITIES: WHAT TO SEE & DO — 14
- 🌐 CIVIC QUARTER 14
  - Leeds Art Gallery 14
- 🌐 EXCHANGE QUARTER 18
  - Leeds Corn Exchange 18
- 🌐 FINANCIAL QUARTER & PARK SQUARE 19
- 🌐 CULTURAL QUARTER 20
  - West Yorkshire Playhouse 20
  - Royal Armouries Museum 20
- 🌐 HISTORICAL LEEDS 23
  - Thackray Medical Museum 23
  - Leeds Industrial Museum at Armley Mills 24
- 🌐 STATELY HOMES 27
  - Temple Newsam 27
  - Harewood House 27
- 🌐 KIRKSTALL ABBEY & ABBEY HOUSE MUSEUM 31
- 🌐 ROUNDHAY PARK 32
- 🌐 SPORT 35

Leeds United (Football) 35
Leeds Rhinos (Rugby) 35

BUDGET TIPS 39

🌐 ACCOMMODATION 39
Premier Inn, City Centre 39
Park Plaza Leeds 40
New Ellington 41
Malmaison Hotel 41
Queens Hotel 42

🌐 PLACES TO EAT 43
Sukhothai South Parade 43
LIVIN'italy 44
Town Hall Tavern 45
Timoney's 45
Sous le Nez en Ville 46

🌐 SHOPPING 47
Briggate 47
Victoria Quarter 48
Kirkgate Market 48
Trinity Leeds Shopping Mall 49
Otley Market 50

🌐 ENTRY REQUIREMENTS 52
Health Insurance 54
Travelling with pets 55

🌐 AIRPORTS, AIRLINES & HUBS 57
Airports 57
Airlines 60
Hubs 62
Sea Ports 62
Eurochannel 64

🌐 MONEY MATTERS 64

Currency 64
Banking/ATMs 65
Credit Cards 65
Tourist Tax..66
Claiming back VAT..66
Tipping Policy 67

CONNECTIVITY 68

Mobile Phones 68
Dialling Code...70
Emergency Numbers 70

GENERAL INFORMATION 71

Public Holidays...71
Time Zone..72
Daylight Savings Time 72
School Holidays..72
Trading Hours...73
Driving Policy...74
Drinking Policy...75
Smoking Policy...75
Electricity..76
Food & Drink..76
Events 79
Websites of Interest 83
Travel Apps 83

LEEDS TRAVEL GUIDE

Leeds

Leeds is one northern England's largest and most important cities. This West Yorkshire city rose to prominence in the 19th century as a major hub of manufacturing and commerce. Its importance during the Industrial Revolution brought jobs, people, and construction to Yorkshire. Some of these buildings exist today which gives the city great architectural character.

LEEDS TRAVEL GUIDE

Like most anywhere in the UK, as you start to explore and peel back the historical layers, you will find evidence of many different eras. Leeds has some of the best-preserved Victorian architecture in England. Stately Tudor homes, medieval monasteries and remnants of the Romans are here. So is Leeds' ultramodern nightlife, great shopping and fantastic food scene.

🌐 Customs & Culture

Leeds takes it's name from the West Yorkshire forest of *Lo* that existed here in the 5th century, and its people were known as Loiners. It's prominence as a leading city is nothing new, as Leeds has been an important market town since the Middle Ages and the Industrial Revolution only magnified its importance. The River Aire and a

LEEDS TRAVEL GUIDE

series of canals made Leeds a good location from which to operate mills and factories with easy transportion options.

Leeds used to produce lots of textiles and clothing, in fact Leeds pioneered the mass production of clothes, much to the chagrin of the tailors and haberdashers of the day. Clothing retail is in the city's blood.

Leeds is a leading city for sports and entertainment. It is home to professional football, rugby and cricket teams. It's a hub for the BBC, which broadcasts its Yorkshire programming from studios located in the city. Leeds boasts two of the UK's leading universities and colleges, an art college and a music conservatory that account for a student population of 200,000 which is the largest in the

UK. With that many young people in one place, there are plenty of options where nightlife is concerned!

The city hosts many festivals that celebrate the arts and the communities that make Leeds such a vibrant and modern metropolis. Its museums are first rate, especially those focused on local history and life in the Victorian era.

🌎 Geography

Leeds is situated on the River Aire and nestled into the foothills of the Pennines. It's just twenty miles away from some of the UK's most beautiful countryside located in the Yorkshire Dales National Park.

Leeds city centre is comprised of four areas: the Civic Quarter, the Financial Quarter, the Cultural Quarter and the Shopping/Exchange Quarter. The city centre is

LEEDS TRAVEL GUIDE

roughly defined within the Leeds Inner Ring Road and is divided in two by the Headrow, a major road that bisects the "inner ring."

Getting to Leeds and getting around is very easy. The Leeds-Bradford International Airport is just ten miles northwest of the city centre. A major train station and bus/coach station is located in the city centre. From there you can travel at all times of the day and most times of the night by ground transportation.

If you're coming from outside Europe you should consider flying into Manchester, as the Leeds-Bradford airport mostly sees arrivals from Europe (and Islamabad, Pakistan with New York flights in the Christmas season).

LEEDS TRAVEL GUIDE

So if you'd rather not have the stress of a layover, fly into Manchester and take one of the trains to Leeds that leave from the airport every half hour (the trip takes 1.5 hours and trains run day and night).

If you're already in the UK, you can take a train from King's Cross Station in London (a 2-2.5 hour trip) or anywhere else, just check the local schedules. National Express and Megabus coaches operate from London Victoria and travel to Leeds often daily.

Leeds is very close to being the geographic centre of Great Britain and it is easily accessibly by road, either by car or by coach from most other large cities.

If you're planning to stay mostly within the city centre, it's recommended that you walk. The city centre is fairly

LEEDS TRAVEL GUIDE

compact, very accessible, and in any case parking a car (and navigating the one-way system) is not always that easy.

If you plan to see more than just the city centre, familiarize yourself with the bus or train service. A MetroDay pass can be purchased for £5.40 and can be used on any West Yorkshire Passenger Transport Authority buses.

Taxis are available and are reasonably priced. Even so, sometimes they're necessary, especially if you're out late (buses/trains stop operating at about 11pm). Try Amber Cabs at 0113-231-1366.

LEEDS TRAVEL GUIDE

🌍 Weather & Best Time to Visit

Leeds has an oceanic climate that is affected by winds off of the Atlantic as they come in contact with the Pennines. This makes for mild summers and winters that are cold, but generally not below freezing. July is the hottest month, with average temperatures ranging from 19.9°C (67.8°F) down to 10.4°C (50.7°F). January is the coldest month when average temperatures dip as low as 0.3°C (32.5°F) but can be as warm as 5.8°C (42.4°F). Although the UK has a reputation for overcast and rainy weather, Leeds is actually one of the driest cities.

The city is great at any time of the year but we'd recommend the summertime (or late-spring/early-autumn). You can time your visit to coincide with one of many festivals, but if you're coming to shop, well, you can come any day of the year. Christmas is, of course, a

LEEDS TRAVEL GUIDE

major shopping season and Leeds goes all out to make it a wonderful experience. The city centre is illuminated with a fantastic light display and German Christmas markets pop up in Millennium Square.

LEEDS TRAVEL GUIDE

LEEDS TRAVEL GUIDE

Sights & Activities: What to See & Do

🌐 Civic Quarter

Leeds Art Gallery

The Headrow

Tel: 0113 247 8256

http://www.leeds.gov.uk/museumsandgalleries/Pages/Leeds-Art-Gallery.aspx

Leeds' Civic Quarter is located in the city centre and – as its name implies – is the municipal heart of the city. Here you'll find the city's Magistrates and Crown courts, as well as the impressive and historic Leeds Town Hall.

The Town Hall is a notable work of Victorian architecture. The neo-classical colonnades of its façade and its looming bell tower hearken back to the early 19th century

LEEDS TRAVEL GUIDE

when Leeds' population was booming due to the Industrial Revolution. Its ancient civic structures were not large enough to accommodate the needs of the city. The Town Hall was built to fix that and was completed by mid-19th century and opened by Queen Victoria.

Today the Town Hall is less of a governmental workplace and more of a cultural venue for concerts and formal functions. Its main hall is a work of art and you should make an effort to see it. The Leeds International Film Festival (held in November) screens movies here and the Leeds International Beer Festival is held here (in September) as well.

The Town Hall also hosts the prestigious Leeds International Piano Competition every three years (next in 2015).

LEEDS TRAVEL GUIDE

Most of the work of running the city is done in Leeds Civic Hall, itself a noteworthy building. Less extravagant, perhaps, than the Town Hall, it is striking nonetheless with its two towers and Georgian façade. It sits behind the Town Hall in Millennium Square.

Millennium Square was created in 2000 by the Millennium Commission to celebrate the millennium. This large public square serves many purposes: as venue for civic ceremonies, major TV sports broadcasts and concerts of all types; a market place, including a popular German Christmas Market; a gathering place to watch major sporting events on a large screen; in winter part of it turns into a skating rink.

LEEDS TRAVEL GUIDE

It is also where Leeds Pride (LGBT) celebration start from on the first Sunday of August. No matter when you visit Leeds, it's very likely that something will be going on in Millennium Square. Bars, restaurants and a theatre line the square.

Also part of Millennium Square is the recently renovated Leeds Art Gallery. This museum is free of charge and exhibits artifacts from Leeds' history, as well as a few other curiosities like the Leeds Mummy and the Leeds Tiger. The Mummy has been in residence at the museum for almost 200 years and is one of the best-preserved Egyptian mummies in Egypt.

The Leeds Tiger has a rather interesting history. It came to the museum as a tigerskin rug during the 19th century and was later combined with a few other pelts to create a

LEEDS TRAVEL GUIDE

reconstructed stuffed tiger. A victim of rather poor taxidermy, the tiger today appears bloated and saggy, but the legends and controversies surrounding it have ensured its permanent display at the museum as it is now much beloved by the people of Leeds. If you're in Millennium Square, you won't want to miss it.

Leeds' Grand Theatre is another landmark building especially if you'd like to see a show. The Victorian building with its gothic towers has been restored to the glory of its heyday as a stage for variety shows that offered a cheaper, bawdier alternative to the opera and theater of high society. Today its ever-changing schedule of shows includes all the best touring productions from the West End, comedy and variety shows, classical works and opera. Eat at the famous Nash's fish and chip

LEEDS TRAVEL GUIDE

restaurant just around the corner after the show (possibly with the actors!)

🌎 Exchange Quarter

Leeds Corn Exchange

Call Lane

Tel: 0113 234 0363

http://www.leedscornexchange.co.uk/

Leeds' Exchange Quarter extends from the Headrow to Boar Lane, and while most of its buildings and venues are covered below in the *Places to Shop* chapter, there are a few places worthy of note as sights to see.

The major landmark of the area is the Corn Exchange that gives the quarter its name. Modeled after the Corn Exchange in Paris, this much-loved circular building is

LEEDS TRAVEL GUIDE

architecturally magnificent and has housed many different operations since its beginning in the Victorian era. There was a time in the mid-20th century that the building fell into disrepair – and with it the neighborhood. It was revived in the 1980s, though, and further renovated in 2007 along with other buildings in the neighborhood so that today it's the centre of a trendy part of town.

The Corn Exchange today is home to a number of boutique shops and cafes and the surrounding area (near the railway station) is full of bars, restaurants and has a bohemian atmosphere, especially at night. When you visit you'll be sure to appreciate the restored beauty and Victorian charm of the area.

🌐 Financial Quarter & Park Square

To the west of the City centre you'll find the Financial Quarter, home to the city's main financial services and law offices. While this is largely a working part of town, it's worth a visit to see Park Square. Located just off of the Headrow, Park Square is a fine example of a Georgian public square. Its many benches provide an excellent place for you to enjoy your lunch, after which you'll want to take a casual stroll through the greenery and admire the fine Georgian buildings that border the small park. These buildings are primarily residential and clerical/legal offices today.

LEEDS TRAVEL GUIDE

🌐 Cultural Quarter

West Yorkshire Playhouse

Playhouse Square, Quarry Hill, Leeds

Tel: 0113 213 770 (box office)

http://www.wyp.org.uk/

Royal Armouries Museum

New Dock (formerly called Clarence Dock)

Armouries Drive, Leeds

Tel: 0113 220 1999

http://www.royalarmouries.org/visit-us/leeds

The city's Cultural Quarter lies to the east and southeast of the city centre (all walking distance, by the way).

LEEDS TRAVEL GUIDE

At the heart of the Cultural Quarter is the West Yorkshire Playhouse, the BBC building and the Leeds College of Music.

The West Yorkshire Playhouse presents an ever-changing repertoire of performances, from Shakespeare to Stephen Sondheim and everything in between. It hosts touring productions and produces regional shows, often with a focus on writers from the north.

The BBC Yorkshire building houses the television and radio studios that produce many of the BBC's programmes in Yorkshire. The top part of their building is a 350-seat auditorium for their neighbor, the Leeds College of Music, which is the UK's largest music conservatory.

LEEDS TRAVEL GUIDE

A bit further south in the Cultural Quarter is the New Dock (formerly Clarence Dock) and the Royal Armouries Museum. This area is a case study in urban revitalization but suffered economically in the recession that started in 2008. New Dock was initially a Victorian canal port that serviced the coal trade, but the advent of railways and (more significantly) road freight led to a slow decline in the area so that by the 1990s there was nothing more than derelict Victorian buildings.

City planners saw the waterfront's potential, however. They built the Royal Armouries Museum and several high-end residential buildings, the result of which is that New Dock is now a rather posh part of town with the promise of excellent shopping and eating. It also hosts an annual Waterfront Festival that showcases a dragon boat race.

LEEDS TRAVEL GUIDE

The large Royal Armouries Museum was built in 1996 along the River Aire to display the National Collection of Arms and Armour, making it a sister museum to the Tower of London. In fact, many pieces of its permanent collection had been sitting in storage at the Tower and were brought to Leeds so that they might have a renewed purpose (beyond simply collecting dust).

A walk through the museum is a walk through over a thousand years of British weaponry and warfare. There are also galleries dedicated to various Asian cultures, hunting, and medieval tournament weapons and armour used in jousting. Finally – perhaps ironically, or perhaps hopeful – there is a Peace Gallery that looks forward to a day when there is no need for any arms of any kind.

LEEDS TRAVEL GUIDE

A particularly novel event series is held in the Royal Armouries Arena: jousting tournaments. Competitors come from all over the world dressed as knights of old and joust on horseback for trophies and honour. If you happen to be in Leeds over Easter weekend or during July/August, you'll definitely want to check this out. Entry is free.

🌐 Historical Leeds

Thackray Medical Museum

141 Beckett St.

Tel: 0113 244 4343

http://www.thackraymedicalmuseum.co.uk/

Leeds Industrial Museum at Armley Mills

Canal Road, Armley (West Leeds)

Tel: 0113 263 7861

http://www.leeds.gov.uk/museumsandgalleries/Pages/armleymills.aspx

The Thackray Medical Museum provides a fascinating – and visceral – study of the history of medicine…and, incidentally, of Leeds and England too.

There are several permanent exhibits to check out – start with *Leeds 1842* which will introduce you to a time early in Queen Victoria's reign when the industrial age was gathering steam and people were flocking to Leeds and other urban centres. TB, cholera and measles tore through the population, especially among the newly

LEEDS TRAVEL GUIDE

arrived workers who lived in cramped conditions. The galleries are set up with realistic scenes for you to walk through and images from Dickens will come to mind.

The museum is housed in a building that was once a Victorian workhouse for the poor, so the pain and sickness you'll come to know through the exhibit would have been prevalent here.

Hannah Dyson's Ordeal will take you back twenty years earlier to show you what happened when Hannah, an 11-year old mill worker, got her leg crushed by a piece of machinery. The surgeon's saved her life – but you'll be thankful that if you suffered the same injury you'd be treated in the 21st century!

LEEDS TRAVEL GUIDE

Pain, Pus and Blood goes even further into the realities of surgery in the Victorian era. No anesthesia. No antiseptics. And a fairly strong chance that after enduring a monstrous amount of pain brought on by surgery, you'd die anyway from blood loss.

These are just a few of the galleries awaiting you and it's all done tastefully.

If your interest is piqued and you are traveling with children, you can take them to the *Life Zone* exhibit. This is a hands-on interactive room that will help kids to learn about their bones, brain and organs in a fun manner.

For more about Victorian Leeds, check out the Leeds Industrial Museum. It's housed in Armley Mills, once the world's largest woollen mill, and it invites the visitor into the world of the 19th century textile worker. Workrooms are set up as they would have been for the average worker, and galleries display the machinery and tools that went into the modernization of Leeds and the clothing industry.

Many visitors describe this museum as one of Leeds hidden gems. Although not terribly difficult to reach, it isn't in the city centre – but given its praise as one of the best and most unique museums, it'll be worth your time to visit.

🌍 Stately Homes

Temple Newsam

Selby Road, Leeds LS15 0AD

http://www.leeds.gov.uk/museumsandgalleries/Pages/Te

LEEDS TRAVEL GUIDE

mple-Newsam.aspx

Tel: 0113 336 7560

Harewood House

Harewood, Leeds, West Yorkshire LS17 9LG

Tel: 0113 218 1010

http://www.harewood.org/

The area surrounding Leeds has a number of stately homes, several of which are of major interest beyond their local relevance.

The first of these is Temple Newsam, east of the city. The house's origins go back to the Tudor period in the early 1500s and if its walls could talk they'd tell quite a story. One of its owners was executed for treason. Another married Mary, Queen of Scots. A daughter of the

LEEDS TRAVEL GUIDE

household was mistress to King George IV (who made a gift of several tapestries which are on display to this day).

In the 18th century, its lands were given a makeover by Capability Brown, who is considered one of England's greatest gardeners. He designed more than 170 gardens and parks. His design is still intact and carefully cultivated.

Today the house is owned and managed by the Leeds City Council, which has converted the home into a top-rate museum and concert/festival venue. Its collection of decorative arts is considered to be of national importance, and as a site for historical research it is considered to be top-notch – in fact, a former cultural minister deemed it one of the top three non-national museums in Britain.

LEEDS TRAVEL GUIDE

Take a look around the house and have a walk around the beautiful grounds. You'll come across the Home Farm, a barn built at the end of the 17th century that today is home to many rare breeds of cattle, sheep and goats. You'll also find sport fields set up to play football, trails for running, cycling and horseback riding.

If you're visiting in July you might want to attend one of two major music festivals. Opera in the Park is an event that brings together major soloists and performers from the world of classical music. They perform an evening of arias, choruses and orchestral works from a selection of different operas. Thousands attend and picnic in the grounds. Sometimes in the rain.

This concert is followed by Party in the Park (the stage and seating are already set up and they are used for a

LEEDS TRAVEL GUIDE

second concert festival the next day). This is a Pop/Rock/Dance music event that attracts around 70,000 young people each year. Both events used to be free, but due to budgetary cuts they now charge a fee – even so, £10 is a reasonable price for an entire day of first-class music.

Harewood House, though 250 years younger than Temple Newsam, is certainly no less grand. Although still a privately owned by the Lascelle family, most of its rooms and the surrounding land are open to the public. On exhibition inside the house are collections of Italian Renaissance paintings by several masters, a modern art collection and a vast array of antique Chippendale furniture and sculpture, as well as several temporary exhibitions.

LEEDS TRAVEL GUIDE

The grounds, as at Temple Newsam, were designed by Capability Brown. The 100 acres include plants from all over the world, a formal Terrace garden, a Himalayan garden and a Bird Garden. The Bird Garden gives refuge for many species of endangered birds (and some that are nearing endangered status). You'll find parrots, flamingos, cranes, owls – and a beloved community of penguins. It's a small zoo.

A walk through the grounds will also lead you to the ancient ruins of the medieval Harewood Castle and All Saints Church. The church was built during the 15th century and it contains the largest collection of alabaster tombs outside of a cathedral.

LEEDS TRAVEL GUIDE

🌐 Kirkstall Abbey & Abbey House Museum

Abbey Walk

Tel: 0113 230 5492

http://www.leeds.gov.uk/museumsandgalleries/Pages/Abbey-House-Museum.aspx

Kirkstall Abbey was founded by Cistercian monks in the 12th century, but came to ruin after Henry VIII's historic dissolution of the monasteries in 1539. Like several other ruined abbeys (e.g. Tintern, Glastonbury) it has, ironically, taken on new life as a ruin thanks to the contributions of artists, poets and generations of visitors who come to see the stunning medieval architecture.

Kirkstall Abbey is more complete than any of the other remaining Cistercian Abbeys (including Tintern). Since they were built to the same architectural plan, historians are able to piece together what these complexes looked like during the height of their glory, and how they functioned as part of ancient British society. You don't have to be an academic, however, to appreciate the quiet and contemplative atmosphere the abbey provides.

The abbey's visitor centre provides context for understanding the lives of the monks who lived there. Nearby, the very interesting Abbey House Museum gives a sense of what life was like in Leeds during the Victorian era. Street scenes are recreated on the ground floor; the galleries upstairs are dedicated to the abbey, social history of the area, and childhood. This is a great museum to bring the kids.

LEEDS TRAVEL GUIDE

🌑 Roundhay Park

You can't visit Leeds and miss out on Roundhay Park. Covering over 700 acres, this is one of the largest city parks in Europe, and with almost a million visitors every year it's one of Leeds' most popular attractions. New York City's Central Park covers 840 acres, so Roundhay approaches its size. There are many unique sights to see tucked away here and there. Here are a few you won't want to miss.

Leeds is very proud of Roundhay Park's HESCO Garden, which won a gold medal from the Chelsea Flower Show. This garden was designed to showcase the role that water played during the industrial revolution and its use as a source of renewable energy today. The garden's centerpiece is a traditional regional mill with a working water wheel.

LEEDS TRAVEL GUIDE

The Canal Gardens sit along a long, rectangular lake (that resembles a canal) and consists of three distinct gardens. The Monet Garden's blooms evoke the impressionist's garden paintings with their many colours. The Alhambra Garden is so named because its fountains and water features are similar to those found at the Alhambra in Granada, Spain. The Friends Garden is planted with fragrant flowers that were picked specifically to create a sensory-rich experience for the blind.

Inside the Canal Gardens area you'll find Tropical World, a greenhouse conservatory that exhibits the second largest collection of tropical plants in the UK. It also has a butterfly house and several aquariums, free ranging birds and lizards, and a family of meerkats that is very popular.

LEEDS TRAVEL GUIDE

Tropical World is particularly recommended during wintertime given its warm temperature.

The Arena is a large track and field where you might see a game of cricket being played. Because the Arena can be set up to seat over 100,000 people, it has also been used as a site for major concerts (from the likes of Genesis, Michael Jackson, U2 and Madonna).

There are two lakes in the park. Upper Lake is the smaller and is so named because it sits on higher ground. It has some lovely fountains, and, due to its higher altitude, a waterfall that flows through a ravine into Waterloo Lake. This lake got its name from the men who built it: unemployed veterans who had helped to defeat Napoleon at Waterloo.

LEEDS TRAVEL GUIDE

The Mansion sits uphill with a view of the Upper Lake. It was once the home of the Nicholson family who owned the land. Today it houses the park's offices as well as a visitor centre and a restaurant. Given its picturesque atmosphere, it has been a popular place for wedding photos – and you'll want to snap a few pics here yourself whether you're getting married or not.

🌎 Sport

Leeds United (Football)

Elland Road Stadium

Tel: 0871 334 1992 (ticket office)

http://www.leedsunited.com/

Leeds Rhinos (Rugby)

Headingley Stadium

Tel: 0871 423 1315 (ticket office)

LEEDS TRAVEL GUIDE

http://www.therhinos.co.uk/

Leeds is a great city for sports, whether you're a spectator or a participant. If you're visiting from outside the UK, you *must* attend a football/soccer game. Whether you're into the sport or not, it's an atmosphere and experience you'll always remember. Leeds United Football Club has been playing at the Elland Road stadium since 1919, and though their heyday was in the 1960s and 1970s, you're still likely to be chanting "*Leeds! Leeds! Leeds!*" with the native Loiners.

Football too hands-off for you? Need something with a little more grit and a bit more bruising? You'll want to check out a game of the Leeds Rhinos, the city's professional rugby team – and the most successful rugby club in the history of Super League competition! You can

LEEDS TRAVEL GUIDE

see them play at Headingley Stadium, which has been their home since 1889. Tickets for either football or rugby can be purchased through the teams' websites.

If you're more interested in being an active participant, any of the parks mentioned are a great place to go and kick a ball around or toss a frisbee. Or you might want to consider playing a round on one of Leeds four 'pay and play' golf courses. Roundhay Park has a 9-hole course (tel: 0113 266 1686). Temple Newsam has two 18-hole courses, both designed by Alistair MacKenzie, the designer of the Augusta National that hosts the US Masters every year (tel: 0113 264 7362). There is an 18-hole course at Middleton Park that offers fantastic views of the city (tel: 0113 270 9506), and one in Gotts Park that is hilly and challenging (tel: 0113 231 1896).

LEEDS TRAVEL GUIDE

A very interesting way to both be active and experience the changing landscape of Leeds is to go for a walk. Well, it's not just any walk. The White Rose Way is a 104-mile walking trail that begins at the Black Prince statue (which you'll find in Leeds City Square near to the Queens Hotel) and goes all the way to Scarborough along the coast. The trail passes through the grounds of Harewood House and leads into some of the picturesque villages of Yorkshire. Even if you don't complete all 104 miles (or only complete one or two miles), you can still say that you walked along the White Rose Way – and you will have seen some interesting sightseeing in Leeds along the path. The guide to the walk can be ordered from http://www.whiteroseway.co.uk/.

LEEDS TRAVEL GUIDE

LEEDS TRAVEL GUIDE

Budget Tips

🌍 Accommodation

Premier Inn, City Centre

Wellington St., City Gate

Tel: 0871 527 8582

http://www.premierinn.com/en/hotel/LEETGI/leeds-city-centre?cmp=GLBC

This is one of several Premier Inns in Leeds (there is one in the northern part of the city centre by the Leeds Arena, and three others in West, East and South Leeds). Rooms here are affordable (prices starting at £29), especially considering the central location. Rooms are spacious with king sized beds and include WiFi, hair dryers, coffee makers, TV (with 80 channels) and showers with strong

LEEDS TRAVEL GUIDE

water pressure. All of the Premier Inns include a restaurant and bar that is open to serve every meal.

Park Plaza Leeds

Boar Lane, City Square

Tel: 0844 415 6722

http://www.parkplaza.com/leeds-hotel-gb-ls1-5ns/gbleeds

Park Plaza is located across from the train station, very close to the Shopping Quarter (so if a little "retail therapy" is the reason for your visit, this would be an excellent location for you).

Rates vary depending upon the time of your visit and method of booking (there are excellent deals if you book online through a third party site like booking.com), but you can usually find a room through their website for under £70 – and if you book online there are many deals for less

LEEDS TRAVEL GUIDE

than £100. Rooms come with free WiFi and the hotel has a fitness centre. There is a flashy Asian-Fusion restaurant (Chino Latino) and posh white bar, both of which are worth visiting whether you stay here or not.

New Ellington

23-25a York Place

Tel: 0113 204 2150

http://www.thenewellington.com/

This is an stylish hotel located in the quiet Financial Quarter. As the name suggests, sultry jazz is the theme of their décor, which is expressed through deep reds and rich mahogany in the rooms and in their Gin Garden lounge (offering more than 80 varieties of gin!). Digby's Restaurant presents a menu of innovative culinary delights. Rooms are available for under £100 per night

LEEDS TRAVEL GUIDE

through their website, with even better deals if you look around online. Along with the usual amenities (free WiFi, excellent bathroom facilities), rooms also come equipped with iPod hubs and there are Nintendo Wii and Xbox consoles available to borrow.

Malmaison Hotel

1 Swinegate

Leeds, LS1 4ES

Tel: 084469 30654

http://www.malmaison.com/locations/leeds/

This beautiful hotel is located in the former Leeds City Tramways office building, conveniently situated in south Briggate area of the city. It is in a pleasantly located on a cobbled street and just a short walk away from everything. Some rooms have beautiful River Aire views. Rooms are chic, spacious and comfortable, and if reservations are made in advance, they're right around £100. Amenities include free WiFi, CD players, a digital television, and hair dryers. Their elegant Brasserie features a menu of northern English fare, and their Malbar is a coffeehouse by day and funky lounge by night.

Queens Hotel

City Square

Tel: 0113 243 1323

http://www.qhotels.co.uk/our-locations/the-queens/

The Queens is a beautiful art deco hotel located near the train station right in the centre of Leeds. Their large amount of event space makes this a very popular hotel for weddings and events. Rooms are equipped with WiFi, hair dryer, air conditioner, flat screen TV – and what they

LEEDS TRAVEL GUIDE

refer to as their signature bed with a mattress that is 10 inches thick. If you shop online it's possible to find prices for less than £100 a night.

🌏 Places to Eat

Sukhothai South Parade

15 South Parade

Tel: 0113 242 2795

http://www.sukhothai.co.uk/

Sukhothai is one of the best Thai restaurants in Leeds and the UK! It's head chef and owner came to Yorkshire from Thailand where she ran a successful restaurant in Bangkok for nearly a decade.

She brings that expertise to Sukhothai, where fresh ingredients go into every dish. If you order a la carte the most expensive dishes are the seafood dishes at £16, but most everything else is under £10. They have a variety of other menu options, however: an Express lunch menu, a two course lunch menu, even a pre-theatre menu. If you're fancying Thai, this is the place to come.

LIVIN'italy

Granary Wharf

Tel: 0113 243 0090

http://livinitaly.com/

LIVIN'italy is the only enoteca gastronomica in northern England. What does that mean exactly? Well, an *enoteca* is essentially a wine library, and one that is *gastronomica* also serves food. In this case, very good Italian food that comes highly praised. Main courses range in price from £9.95-£14.50 – and of course you'll want to try something from their wine list, so be sure to ask their sommelier what goes best with your dish. Or you could even skip the meal and go straight to wine and dessert.

Next door "under the arches" is the Hop, a happening bar featuring live music and a pub quiz every Tuesday.

Town Hall Tavern

17 Westgate

Tel: 0113 244 0765

http://www.townhalltavernleeds.co.uk/

The Town Hall Tavern is very close to Park Square and specializes in traditional Yorkshire fare – from classic entrees to guilt-inducing comfort food – using only the best ingredients from the region. Prices range from £6-

LEEDS TRAVEL GUIDE

£18 with most dishes around £10. If you're around on a Sunday, stop by to try out something from their Sunday roast menu (served from 12:00-4:30pm).

Timoney's

647 Roundhay Road

Leeds LS8 4BA

Tel: 0113 248 8333

At the southernmost point of Roundhay Park you'll find Timoney's, highly praised for its delicious brunch menu (and it's open for dinner, too), and even more so for its wonderfully warm and attentive staff. It's so popular that you might want to book ahead early. Prices are reasonable – brunch for two comes to about £24 (including coffee).

LEEDS TRAVEL GUIDE

Sous le Nez en Ville

The Basement, Quebec House

Quebec Street

Leeds City Centre

Tel: 0113 244 0108

http://www.souslenez.com/

Sous le Nez, as you might have guessed from the name, is a French restaurant located at the edge of the Financial Quarter. The cuisine is both expertly prepared traditional French as well as French with a modern European twist. You could order a la carte, but their *menu du soir* includes three courses and half a bottle of wine for only £25.95 -- you can't beat it!

LEEDS TRAVEL GUIDE

🌐 Shopping

Briggate

Leeds' Shopping Quarter (close to the Corn Exchange) extends from the Headrow to Boar Lane and includes a large variety of choices, from the very high-end to the more affordable. Briggate is the nerve centre of the shopping district, and most of the other quarters and arcades connect to it. You'll find just about anything you could need on this pedestrianised retail thoroughfare – including a lot of energy and fun.

Stores here include H&M, Zara, American Apparel and Gap, and there is an assortment of fast food options for shoppers on the go who need a quick bite.

Victoria Quarter

Just off Briggate, to the north

Victoria Quarter represents the higher end of retail – in fact, it's been described as "the Knightsbridge of the North" given that several famous shops that had previously existed only in London opened their first satellite stores in Victoria Quarter (Harvey Nichols, for example). It's worth a walk through even if you only plan to window shop: the quarter is comprised of several beautiful covered arcades (with arched glass ceilings, take your camera), facades tiled with colorful faience, and a lot of Victorian charm. Shops include Diesel, Ugg, Reiss and Louis Vuitton (and this particular LV location was the first to include a VIP area!).

LEEDS TRAVEL GUIDE

Kirkgate Market

Close to Corn Exchange

This is Europe's largest covered market and is housed inside a beautiful and iconic Victorian building. Have a walk around and take in all the sights and smells of the fresh produce and flowers. Explore the many different stalls of unique clothing and jewelry that you won't find in the mass-produced department stores.

Kirkgate Market is also famous for housing the very first Marks & Spencer in the late 19th century. This small, one-cart penny bazaar grew into one of Britain's largest retailers, but its humble beginnings were here in Victorian Leeds. A clock marks the location of that first store, and M&S has reopened a small booth near to it, but if you're

LEEDS TRAVEL GUIDE

looking for the modern location you'll have to head out to Briggate.

Trinity Leeds Shopping Mall

Off Briggate in the City Centre

In March 2013 Leeds' status as a commercial capital was heightened even further with the addition of a brand new shopping centre called Trinity Leeds. This was the largest shopping mall that opened in Europe in 2013, and has over 120 stores, making it one of the Yorkshire's largest shopping areas.

You'll find a huge variety of retailers here (Apple, Fossil, Armani Exchange, Topshop, etc.). There's also an Everyman movie theater if you're feeling the need to sit and relax for two hours after your intense shopping workout. This mall is very active and is much more established than the New Dock shopping area which is 15 minutes walk to the southeast.

Otley Market

Given the number of arcades, shops, markets and malls in the shopping district, there's no need to go anywhere else to shop in Leeds. However, if you'd like to escape the crowds and have a calmer shopping experience, head north to the beautiful, green countryside and town of Otley. This quaint, beautiful Yorkshire market town is part of metropolitan Leeds. Their outdoor market is open from 9:00am-1:00pm every Tuesday, Friday, Saturday and Sunday in Otley town centre. Over 100 stalls are set up, so you'll have a great time meandering aimlessly and chatting with the local vendors. It's just a 30 minute bus ride from the city centre.

LEEDS TRAVEL GUIDE

LEEDS TRAVEL GUIDE

🌐 Entry Requirements

Citizens of the European Union do not need a visa when visiting the UK. Non-EU members from European countries within the European Economic Area (EEA) are also exempt. This includes countries like Iceland, Norway, Liechtenstein and Switzerland. Visitors from Canada, Australia, Japan, Malaysia, Hong Kong SAR, New Zealand, Singapore, South Korea and the USA do not need a visa to visit the UK, provided that their stay does not exceed 6 months. Visitors from Oman, Qatar and the United Arab Emirates may apply for an Electronic Visa Waiver (EVW) via the internet, if their stay in the UK is less than 6 months. You will need a visa to visit the UK, if travelling from India, Jamaica, Cuba, South Africa, Thailand, the People's Republic of China, Saudi Arabia, Zimbabwe, Indonesia, Cambodia, Nigeria, Ghana, Kenya, Egypt, Ethiopia, Vietnam, Turkey, Taiwan, Pakistan, Russia, the Philippines, Iran, Afghanistan and more. If you are in doubt about the status of your country, do inquire with officials of the relevant UK Embassy, who should be able to advise you. Visitors from the EU (European Union) or EEA (European Economic Area) will not require immigration clearance when staying in the Isle of Man, but may require a work permit if they wish to take employment there. If needed, a visa for the Isle of Man may be obtained from the British Embassy or High Commission in your country. Applications can be made via the Internet.

LEEDS TRAVEL GUIDE

If you wish to study in the UK, you will need to qualify for a student visa. There are a number of requirements. First, you have to provide proof of acceptance into an academic institution and available funding for tuition, as well as monthly living costs. A health surcharge of £150 will be levied for access to the National Health Service. Applications can be made online and will be subject to a points based evaluation system.

If you need to visit the UK for professional reasons, there are several different classes of temporary work visas. Charity volunteers, sports professionals and creative individuals can qualify for a stay of up to 12 months, on submission of a certificate of sponsorship. Nationals from Canada, Australia, Japan, Monaco, New Zealand, Hong Kong, Taiwan and the Republic of Korea can also apply for the Youth Mobility Scheme that will allow them to work in the UK for up to two years, if they are between the ages of 18 and 30. Citizens of Commonwealth member countries may qualify for an ancestral visa that will enable them to stay for up to 5 years and apply for an extension.

LEEDS TRAVEL GUIDE

Health Insurance

Visitors from the European Union or EEA (European Economic Area) countries are covered for using the UK's National Health Service, by virtue of a European Health Insurance Card (EHIC). This includes visitors from Switzerland, Liechtenstein, the Canary Islands and Iceland. The card can be applied for free of charge. If you are in doubt about the process, the European Commission has created phone apps for Android, IPhone and Windows to inform European travellers about health matters in various different countries.

Bear in mind that a slightly different agreement is in place for Crown Dependencies, such as the Isle of Man and the Channel Islands. There is a reciprocal agreement between the UK and the Isle of Man with regards to basic healthcare, but this does not include the option of repatriation, which could involve a considerable expense, should facilities such as an Air Ambulance be required. If visiting the UK from the Isle of Man, do check the extent of your health insurance before your departure. A similar reciprocal agreement exists between the UK and the Channel Islands. This covers basic emergency healthcare, but it is recommended that you inquire about travel health insurance if visiting the UK from the Channel Islands.

LEEDS TRAVEL GUIDE

The UK has a reciprocal healthcare agreement with several countries including Australia, New Zealand, Barbados, Gibraltar, the Channel Islands, Montserrat, Romania, Turkey, Switzerland, the British Virgin Islands, the Caicos Islands, Bulgaria, the Falkland Islands and Anguilla, which means that nationals of these countries are covered when visiting the UK. In some cases, only emergency care is exempted from charges. Reciprocal agreements with Armenia, Azerbaijan, Belarus, Georgia, Kazakhstan, Kyrgyzstan, Moldova, Russia, Tajikistan, Turkmenistan, Ukraine and Uzbekistan were terminated at the beginning of 2016 and no longer apply.

Visitors from non European countries without medical insurance will be charged 150 percent of the usual rate, should they need to make use of the National Health Service (NHS). Exemptions exist for a number of categories, including refugees, asylum seekers. Anyone with a British work permit is also covered for health care. Find out the extent of your health cover before leaving home and make arrangements for adequate travel insurance, if you need additional cover.

Travelling with pets

If travelling from another country within the EU, your pet will be able to enter the UK without quarantine, provided that

LEEDS TRAVEL GUIDE

certain entry requirements are met. The animal will need to be microchipped and up to date on rabies vaccinations. This means that the vaccinations should have occurred no later than 21 days before your date of departure. In the case of dogs, treatment against tapeworm must also be undertaken before your departure. You will need to carry an EU pet passport. If travelling from outside the EU, a third-country official veterinary certificate will need to be issued within 10 days of your planned departure. Check with your vet or the UK embassy in your country about specific restrictions or requirements for travel with pets.

In the case of cats travelling from Australia, a statement will need to be issued by the Australian Department of Agriculture to confirm that your pet has not been in contact with carriers of the Hendra virus. If travelling from Malaysia, you will need to carry documentation from a vet that your pet has tested negative for the Nipah virus within 10 days before your departure. There are no restrictions on pet rodents, rabbits, birds, reptilians, fish, amphibians or reptiles, provided that they are brought from another EU country. For pet rabbits and rodents from countries outside the European Union, a four month quarantine period will be required, as well as a rabies import licence. Entry is prohibited for prairie dogs from the USA and squirrels and rodents from sub-Saharan Africa.

LEEDS TRAVEL GUIDE

🌍 Airports, Airlines & Hubs

Airports

London, the capital of England and the UK's most popular tourist destination is served by no less than 6 different airports. Of these, the best known is **Heathrow International Airport (LHR)**, which ranks as the busiest airport in the UK and Europe and sixth busiest in the world. Heathrow is located about 23km to the west of the central part of London. It is utilized by more than 90 airlines and connects to 170 destinations around the world. The second busiest is **Gatwick Airport (LGW)**, which lies 5km north of Crawley and about 47km south of the central part of London. Its single runway is the world's busiest and in particular, it offers connections to the most popular European destinations. From 2013, it offered travellers a free flight connection service, called Gatwick Connect if the service is not available through their individual airlines. **London Luton Airport (LTN)** is located less than 3km from Luton and about 56km north of London's city center. It is the home of EasyJet, the UK's largest airline, but also serves as a base for Monarch, Thomson Airlines and Ryanair. **London Stansted Airport (STN)** is the fourth busiest airport in the UK. Located about 48km northeast of London, it is an important base for Ryanair and also utilized by EasyJet, Thomas Cook Airline and Thomson Airways. **London Southend Airport (SEN)** is

LEEDS TRAVEL GUIDE

located in Essex, about 68km from London's central business area. Once the third busiest airport in London, it still handles air traffic for EasyJet and Flybe. Although **City Airport (LCY)** is the nearest to the city center of London, its facilities are compact and limiting. The short runway means that it is not really equipped to handle large aircraft and the airport is not operational at night either. It is located in the Docklands area, about 6.4km from Canary Wharf and mainly serves business travellers. Despite these restrictions, it is still the 5th busiest airport in London and 13th busiest in Europe.

The UK's third busiest airport is **Manchester International Airport (MAN)**, which is located about 13.9km southwest of Manchester's CBD. **Birmingham Airport (BHX)** is located 10km from Birmingham's CBD and offers connections to domestic as well as international destinations. **Newcastle International Airport (NCL)** is located about 9.3km from Newcastle's city center and offers connections to Tyne and Wear, Northumberland, Cumbria, North Yorkshire and even Scotland. **Leeds/Bradford Airport (LBA)** provides connections to various cities in the Yorkshire area, including Leeds, Bradford, York and Wakefield. **Liverpool International Airport (LPL)**, also known as Liverpool John Lennon Airport, serves the north-western part of England and provides connections to destinations in Germany, France, Poland, the Netherlands, Spain, Greece, Cyprus, the USA, the Canary

LEEDS TRAVEL GUIDE

Islands, Malta, Jersey and the Isle of Man. **Bristol Airport (BRS)** provides international access to the city of Bristol, as well as the counties of Somerset and Gloucestershire. As the 9th busiest airport in the UK, it also serves as a base for budget airlines such as EasyJet and Ryanair. **East Midlands Airport (EMA)** connects travellers to Nottingham.

Edinburgh Airport (EDI) is the busiest in Scotland and one of the busier airports in the UK. Its primary connections are to London, Bristol, Birmingham, Belfast, Amsterdam, Paris, Frankfurt, Dublin and Geneva. Facilities include currency exchange, a pet reception center and tourist information desk. **Glasgow International Airport (GLA)** is the second busiest airport in Scotland and one of the 10 busiest airports of the UK. As a gateway to the western part of Scotland, it also serves as a primary airport for trans-Atlantic connections to Scotland and as a base for budget airlines such as Ryanair, Flybe, EasyJet and Thomas Cook. **Cardiff Airport (CWL)** lies about 19km west of the city center of Cardiff and provides access to Cardiff, as well as the south, mid and western parts of Wales. In particular, it offers domestic connections to Glasgow, Edinburgh, Belfast, Aberdeen and Newcastle. **Belfast International Airport (BFS)** is the gateway to Northern Ireland and welcomes approximately 4 million passengers per year. **Kirkwall Airport (KOI)** was originally built for use by the RAF in 1940, but reverted to civilian aviation from 1948. It is located near the town of

LEEDS TRAVEL GUIDE

Kirkwall and serves as gateway to the Orkney Islands. It is mainly utilized by the regional Flybe service and the Scottish airline, Loganair. The airports at **Guernsey (GCI)** and **Jersey (JER)** offer access to the Channel Islands.

Airlines

British Airways (BA) is the UK's flag carrier airline and was formed around 1972 from the merger of British Overseas Airways Corporation (BOAC) and British European Airways (BEA). It has the largest fleet in the UK and flies to over 160 destinations on 6 different continents. A subsidiary, BA CityFlyer, manages domestic and European connections. British Airways Limited maintains an executive service linking London to New York. The budget airline EasyJet is based at London Luton Airport. In terms of annual passenger statistics, it is Britain's largest airline and Europe's second largest airline after Ryanair. With 19 bases around Europe, it fosters strong connections with Italy, France, Germany and Spain. Thomas Cook Airlines operates as the air travel division of the Thomas Cook group, Britain and the world's oldest travel agent. Thomson Airways is the world's largest charter airline, resulting from a merger between TUI AG and First Choice Holidays. The brand operates scheduled and chartered flights connecting Ireland and the UK with Europe, Africa, Asia and North

LEEDS TRAVEL GUIDE

America. Founded in the 1960s, Monarch Airlines still operates under the original brand identity and maintains bases at Leeds, Birmingham, Gatwick and Manchester. Its primary base is at London Luton Airport. Jet2.com is a budget airline based at Leeds/Bradford, which offers connections to 57 destinations. Virgin Atlantic, the 7th largest airline in the UK, operates mainly from its bases at Heathrow, Gatwick and Manchester Airport.

Flybe is a regional, domestic service which provides connections to UK destinations. Covering the Channel Islands, Flybe is in partnership with Blue Islands, an airline based on the island of Guernsey. Blue Islands offers connections from Guernsey to Jersey, London, Southampton, Bristol, Dundee, Zurich and Geneva. Loganair is a regional Scottish airline which is headquartered at Glasgow International Airport. It provides connections to various destinations in Scotland, including Aberdeen, Edinburgh, Inverness, Norwich and Dundee. Additionally it operates a service to the Shetland Islands, the Orkney Islands and the Western Islands in partnership with Flybe. BMI Regional, also known as British Midland Regional Limited, is based at East Midlands Airport and offers connections to other British destinations such as Aberdeen, Bristol and Newcastle, as well as several cities in Europe.

LEEDS TRAVEL GUIDE

Hubs

Heathrow Airport serves as a primary hub for British Airways. Gatwick Airport serves as a hub for British Airways and EasyJet. EasyJet is based at London Luton Airport, but also maintains a strong presence at London's Stansted Airport and Bristol Airport. Manchester Airport serves as a hub for the regional budget airline Flybe, as does Birmingham Airport. Thompson Airways maintain bases at three of London's airports, namely Gatwick, London Luton and Stansted, as well as Belfast, Birmingham, Bournemouth, Bristol, Cardiff, Doncaster/Sheffield, East Midlands, Edinburgh, Exeter, Glasgow, Leeds/Bradford, Manchester and Newcastle. Jet2.com has bases at Leeds/Bradford, Belfast, East Midlands, Edinburgh, Glasgow, Manchester and Newcastle. Glasgow International Airport serves as the primary hub for the Scottish airline, Loganair, which also has hubs at Edinburgh, Dundee, Aberdeen and Inverness.

Sea Ports

As the nearest English port to the French coast, Dover in Kent has been used to facilitate Channel crossings to the European mainland for centuries. This makes it one of the busiest passenger ports in the world. Annually, 16 million passengers,

LEEDS TRAVEL GUIDE

2.8 million private vehicles and 2.1 million trucks pass through its terminals. Three ferry services to France are based on the Eastern dock, connecting passengers to ports in Calais and Dunkirk. Additionally, the Port of Dover also has a cruise terminal, as well as a marina.

The Port of Southampton is a famous port on the central part of the south coast of the UK. It enjoys a sheltered location thanks to the proximity of the Isle of Wight and a tidal quirk that favours its facilities for bulky freighters as well as large cruise liners. The port serves as a base for several UK cruise operators including Cunard, Celebrity Cruises, P&O Cruises, Princess Cruises and Royal Caribbean. Other tour operators using its terminals include MSC Cruises, Costa Cruises, Crystal Cruises and Fred. Olsen Cruise Lines. Southampton is a popular departure point for various cruises to European cities such as Hamburg, Rotterdam, Amsterdam, Le Havre, Bruges, Barcelona, Lisbon, Genoa and Scandinavia, as well as trans-Atlantic destinations such as Boston, New York and Miami. A short but popular excursion is the two day cruise to Guernsey. Southampton also offers ferry connections to the Isle of Wight and the village of Hythe. The port has four cruise terminals and is well-connected by rail to London and other locations in the UK.

LEEDS TRAVEL GUIDE

Eurochannel

The Eurotunnel (or the Channel Tunnel) was completed in 1994 and connects Folkestone in Kent with Coquelles near Calais. This offers travellers a new option for entering the UK from the European continent. Via the Eurostar rail network, passengers travelling to or from the UK are connected with destinations across Europe, including Paris, Brussels, Frankfurt, Amsterdam and Geneva. On the UK side, it connects to the London St Pancras station. Also known as St Pancras International, this station is one of the UK's primary terminals for the Eurostar service. The Eurotunnel Shuttle conveys private and commercial vehicles through the tunnel and provides easy motorway access on either side.

Money Matters

Currency

The currency of the UK is the Pound Sterling. Notes are issued in denominations of £5, £10, £20 and £50. Coins are issued in denominations of £2, £1, 50p, 20p, 10p, 5p, 2p and 1p. Regional variants of the pound are issued in Scotland and Northern Ireland, but these are acceptable as legal tender in other parts of the UK as well. The Isles of Jersey, Guernsey and

LEEDS TRAVEL GUIDE

Man issue their own currency, known respectively as the Jersey Pound, the Guernsey Pound and the Manx Pound. However, the Pound Sterling (and its Scottish and Northern Irish variants) can also be used for payment on the Isle of Man, Jersey and Guernsey.

Banking/ATMs

ATM machines, also known locally as cashpoints or a hole in the wall, are well distributed in cities and larger towns across the UK. Most of these should be compatible with your own banking network, and may even be enabled to give instructions in multiple languages. A small fee is charged per transaction. Beware of helpful strangers, tampering and other scams at ATM machines. Banking hours vary according to bank group and location, but you can generally expect trading hours between 9.30am and 4.30pm.

Credit Cards

Credit cards are widely accepted at many businesses in the UK, but you may run into smaller shops, restaurants and pubs that do not offer credit card facilities. Cash is still king in the British pub, although most have adapted to credit card use. For hotel bookings or car rentals, credit cards are essential. Visa and MasterCard are most commonly used. Acceptance of American Express and Diners Club is less widespread. Chip and PIN cards are the norm in the UK. While shops will generally have card facilities that can still accept older magnetic strip or US chip-and-signature cards, you will find that ticket machines and self service vendors are not configured for those types of credit cards.

Tourist Tax

A tourist tax of £1 for London has been under discussion, but to date nothing has been implemented. The areas of Cornwall, Brighton, Edinburgh, Westminster and Birmingham also considered implementing a tourist tax, but eventually rejected the idea.

Claiming back VAT

If you are not from the European Union, you can claim back VAT (or Value Added Tax) paid on your purchases in the UK. The VAT rate in the UK is 20 percent, but to qualify for a refund, certain conditions will have to be met. Firstly, VAT can only be claimed merchants participating in a VAT refund

LEEDS TRAVEL GUIDE

program scheme. If this is indicated, you can ask the retailer for a VAT 407 form. You may need to provide proof of eligibility by producing your passport. Customs authorities at your point of departure from the European Union (this could be the UK or another country) will inspect the completed form as well as your purchased goods. You should receive your refund from a refund booth at the airport or from the refund department of the retailer where you bought the goods.

Tipping Policy

It is customary to tip for taxis, restaurants and in bars where you are served by waiting staff, rather than bartenders. The usual rate is between 10 and 15 percent. Some restaurants will add this automatically to your bill as a service charge, usually at a rate of 12.5 percent. Tipping is not expected in most pubs, although you may offer a small sum (traditionally the price of a half pint), with the words "and have one yourself". Some hotels will also add a service charge of between 10 and 15 percent to your bill. You may leave a tip for room-cleaning staff upon departure. Tip bellboys and porters to express your gratitude for a particular service, such as helping with your luggage or organizing a taxi or booking a tour. Tipping is not expected at fast food, self service or takeaway outlets, but if the food is delivered, do tip the delivery person. You may also tip a tour guide between £2 and £5 per person, or £1 to £2 if part of a family group, especially if the person was attentive, engaging and knowledgeable. In Scotland, most restaurants do not levy a service charge and it is customary to tip between 10 and 15 percent. Tipping in Scottish pubs is not necessary, unless you were served a meal.

Connectivity

Mobile Phones

Like most EU countries, the UK uses the GSM mobile service. This means that visitors from the EU should have no problem using their mobile phones, when visiting the UK. If visiting from the USA, Canada, Japan, India, Brazil or South Korea, you should check with your service provider about compatibility and roaming fees. The US service providers Sprint, Verizon and U.S. Cellular employ the CDMA network, which is not compatible with the UK's phone networks. Even if your phone does use the GSM service, you will still incur extra costs, if using your phone in the UK. For European visitors the rates will vary from 28p per minute for voice calls and 58p per megabyte for data. The alternative option would be to purchase a UK sim card to use during your stay in the UK. It is relatively easy to get a SIM card, though. No proof of identification or

LEEDS TRAVEL GUIDE

address details will be required and the SIM card itself is often free, when combined with a top-up package.

The UK has four mobile networks. They are Vodafone, O2, Three (3) and EE (Everything Everywhere), the latter of which grew from a merger between Orange and T-Mobile. All of these do offer pay-as-you-go packages that are tailor made for visitors. Through EE, you will enjoy access to a fast and efficient 4G network, as well as 3G and 2G coverage. There is a whole range of pay as you go products, which are still part of the Orange brand. These have been named after different animals, each with a different set of rewards. The dolphin package, which includes free internet and free texts will seem ideal to most tech savvy travellers. The canary plan offers free calls, texts and photo messages, while the raccoon offers the lowest call rate. Also through EE, you can choose from three different package deals, starting from as little as £1 and choose whether to favour data or call time.

With the Three packages, you will get a free SIM with the All-in-One package of £10. Your rewards will include a mix of 500Mb data, 3000 texts and 100 minutes calltime. It is valid for 30 days. Through the O2 network, you can get a free SIM card, when you choose from a selection of different top-up packages, priced from £10. As a service provider, O2 also offers users an international SIM card, which will enable you to call and text

LEEDS TRAVEL GUIDE

landline as well as mobile numbers in over 200 countries. With Vodafone, you can choose between a mixed top-up package that adds the reward of data to the benefit of voice calls and data only SIM card offer. The packages start at £10.

Alternately, you could also explore the various offers from a range of virtual suppliers, which include Virgin Mobile, Lebara Mobile, Lycamobile, Post Office Mobile and Vectone Mobile. Virtual Packages are also available through the retailers Tesco and ASDA.

Dialling Code

The international dialling code for the UK is +44.

Emergency Numbers

General Emergency: 999
(The European Union General emergency number of 112 can also be accessed in the UK. Calls will be answered by 999 operators)
National Health Service (NHS): 111
Police (non-emergency): 101

MasterCard: 0800 056 0572

Visa: 0800 015 0401

🌐 General Information

Public Holidays

1 January: New Year's Day (if New Year's Day falls on a Saturday or Sunday, the 2nd or 3rd of January may also be declared a public holiday).

17 March: St Patrick's Day (Northern Ireland only)

March/April: Good Friday

March/April: Easter Monday

First Monday in May: May Day Bank Holiday

Last Monday in May: Spring Bank Holiday

12 July: Battle of the Boyne/Orangemen's Day (North Ireland only)

First Monday of August: Summer Bank Holiday (Scotland only)

Last Monday of August: Summer Bank Holiday (everywhere in the UK, except Scotland)

30 November: St Andrew's Day (Scotland only)

25 December: Christmas Day

26 December: Boxing Day

LEEDS TRAVEL GUIDE

(if Christmas Day or Boxing Day falls on a Saturday or Sunday, 27 and/or 28 December may also be declared a public holiday)

Time Zone

The UK falls in the Western European Time Zone. This can be calculated as Greenwich Mean Time/Co-ordinated Universal Time (GMT/UTC) 0 in winter and +1 in summer for British Summer Time.

Daylight Savings Time

Clocks are set forward one hour at 01.00am on the last Sunday of March and set back one hour at 02.00am on the last Sunday of October for Daylight Savings Time.

School Holidays

In the UK, school holidays are determined by city or regional authorities. This means that it could vary from town to town, but general guidelines are followed. There are short breaks to coincide with Christmas and Easter, as well as short mid terms for winter (in February), summer (around June) and autumn (in

LEEDS TRAVEL GUIDE

October). A longer summer holiday at the end of the academic year lasts from mid July to the end of August.

Trading Hours

For large shops, trading hours will depend on location. There are outlets for large supermarket chains such as Asda and Tesco that are open round the clock on weekdays or may trade from 6am to 11pm. In England and Wales, the regulations on Sunday trading are set according the size of the shop. While there are no restrictions on shops less than 280 square meters, shops above that size are restricted to 6 hours trading on Sundays and no trading on Christmas or Easter Sunday. Post office trading hours vary according to region and branch. Most post offices are open 7 days a week, but hours may differ according to location.

In Scotland, the trading hours for most shops are from 9am to 5pm, Monday to Saturdays. In larger towns, urban city areas and villages frequented by tourists, many shops will elect to trade on Sundays as well. Some rural shops will however close at 1am on a weekday, which would usually be Wednesday or Thursday. Some shops have introduced late trading hours on Thursdays and longer trading hours may also apply in the summer months and in the run-up to Christmas. On the Scottish

LEEDS TRAVEL GUIDE

islands of Lewis, Harris and North Uist, all shops will be closed on a Sunday.

Driving Policy

In the UK, driving is on the left side of the road. Both front and rear passengers must wear seat belts. If travelling with children, they must be accommodated with an age-appropriate child seat. With rental cars, it is advisable to make prior arrangements for this when you arrange your booking. If stopped by the police, you may be asked for your driver's licence, insurance certificate and MOT certificate, which must be rendered within 7 days. Driving without insurance could result in the confiscation of your vehicle.

In urban and residential areas, the speed limit for all types of vehicles is 48km per hour. On motorways and dual carriageways, cars, motorcycles and motor homes less than 3.05 tonnes are allowed to drive up to 112km per hour. On a single carriageway, this drops to 96km per hour. For motorhomes above 3.05 tonnes and vehicles towing caravans or trailers, the speed limit is 80km for single carriageways and 96km for dual carriageways and motorways. Local speed limits may vary. The alcohol limit for drivers is 35mg per 100ml of breath in England

and Wales and 22mg per 100ml of breath in Scotland (or 80mg and 50mg respectively per 100ml of blood).

Drinking Policy

The legal age for buying alcohol in the UK is 18. Young persons of 16 to 17 may drink a single beer, cider or glass of wine in a pub, provided they are in the company of an adult. From the age of 14, persons can enter a pub unaccompanied to enjoy a meal and children are allowed in pubs with their parents until 9pm. For buying alcohol at an off-license, you will need to be over 21 and may be asked to provide identification.

Smoking Policy

In the UK, smoking is prohibited in public buildings, all enclosed spaces and on public transport. Smoking is also prohibited at bus shelters. The law also states that 'no smoking' signage must be displayed clearly within all premises covered by the legislation. The only exceptions are rooms specifically designated as smoking rooms.

LEEDS TRAVEL GUIDE

Electricity

Electricity: 230 volts

Frequency: 50 Hz

The UK's electricity sockets are compatible with the Type G plugs, a plug that features three rectangular pins or prongs, arranged in a triangular shape. They are incompatible with the two pronged Type C plugs commonly used on the European continent, as UK sockets are shuttered and will not open without the insertion of the third "earth" pin. If travelling from the USA, you will need a power converter or transformer to convert the voltage from 230 to 110, to avoid damage to your appliances. The latest models of certain types of camcorders, cell phones and digital cameras are dual-voltage, which means that they were manufactured with a built in converter, but you will have to check with your dealer about that.

Food & Drink

England gave the world one of its favourite breakfast, the Full English, a hearty feast of bacon eggs, sausage, fried mushroom and grilled tomato. In the UK, this signature dish is incomplete without a helping of baked beans. In Scotland, you can expect to see black pudding or Lorne sausage added to the ensemble, while the Welsh often throw in some cockles or Laverbread.

LEEDS TRAVEL GUIDE

For simple, basic meals, you cannot go wrong with traditional pub fare. All round favourites include the beef pie, shepherd's pie, bangers and mash and toasted sandwiches. Fish and chips, served in a rolled up sheet of newsprint, is another firm favourite. For Sunday roast, expect an elaborate spread of roasted meat, roasted potatoes, vegetables and Yorkshire pudding. The national dish of Scotland is, of course, Haggis - sheep's offal which is seasoned and boiled in a sheep's stomach. This dish rises to prominence on Burns Night (25 January), when the birthday of the poet Robert Burns is celebrated. Burns wrote 'Address to a Haggis'. The influence of immigrants to the UK has led to kosher haggis (which is 100 percent free of pork products) and an Indian variant, Haggis pakora, said to have originated from the Sikh community. The synergy of Anglo-Indian cuisine also gave rise to popular dishes such as Chicken Tikka Masala and Kedgeree.

The neighbourhood pub is an integral part of social life in the UK and Britain is known for its dark ale, also referred to as bitter. Currently, the most popular beer in the UK is Carling, a Canadian import which has available in the British Isles since the 1980s. Foster's Lager, the second most popular beer in the UK, is brewed by Scottish & Newcastle, the largest brewery in Britain. For a highly rated local brew, raise a mug of award-winning Fuller's beer. The brewery was established early in the 1800s and produces London Pride, London Porter and Chiswick

LEEDS TRAVEL GUIDE

Bitter, to name just a few. A popular brand from neighbouring Ireland is Guinness. Along with Indian curries, the market share of Indian beer brands like Jaipur or Cobra beer has grown in recent years. Kent has developed as an emergent wine producer.

On the non-alcoholic side, you can hardly beat tea for popularity. The English like to brew it strong and serve it in a warmed china teapot with generous amounts of milk. Tea is served at 11am and 4pm. Afternoon tea is often accompanied with light snacks, such as freshly baked scones or cucumber sandwiches. High tea, served a little later at 6pm, can be regarded as a meal. A mixture of sweet and savoury treats such as cakes, scones, crumpets, cheese or poached egg on toast, cold meats and pickles. The custom of High Tea goes back to the days when dinner was the midday meal. These days, it is often replaced by supper.

Scotland is known for producing some of the world's finest whiskies. Its industry goes back at least 500 years. One of Scotland's best selling single malt whisky is produced by the famous Glenmorangie distillery in the Highlands. Chivas Brothers, who once supplied whisky by royal warrant to Queen Victoria's Scottish household, produce Chivas Regal, one of the best known blended whiskies of Scotland. The Famous Grouse, which is based at Glenturret near the Highlands town of Crieff, produces several excellent examples of blended grain whiskies.

LEEDS TRAVEL GUIDE

Bell's Whisky is one of the top selling whiskies in the UK and Europe. Other well known Scottish whisky brands include Old Pulteney, Glen Elgin, Tamdhu (a Speyside distillery that produces single malt), Balvenie, Bunnahabhain, Macallan, Aberlour, Bowmore, the award-winning Ballantine and Grant's whisky, from a distillery that has been run by the same family for five generations. Another proudly Scottish drink is Drambuie, the first liqueur stocked by the House of Lords. According to legend, its recipe was originally gifted to the MacKinnon clan by Bonnie Prince Charlie.

Events

Sports

Horse racing is often called the sport of kings and has enjoyed the support of the British aristocracy for centuries. Here you can expect to rub shoulders with high society and several races go back to the 1700s. The Cheltenham Festival is usually on or near St Patrick's Day and now comprises a four day event of 27 races. The Grand National takes place in Liverpool in April. With prize money of £1 million, this challenging event is Europe's richest steeplechase. A Scottish equivalent of the Grand National takes place in Ayr in the same month. There is

LEEDS TRAVEL GUIDE

also a Welsh Grand National, which now takes place in the winter at Chepstow. A past winner of Welsh event was none other than the author Dick Francis. Other important horse races are the Guineas at Newmarket (April/May), the Epsom Oaks and the Epsom Derby (first Saturday of June) and the St Leger Stakes, which takes place in Doncaster in September. One of the annual highlights is Royal Ascot week, traditionally attended by the British Royal Family. This takes place in June at Berkshire. There is a strict dress code and access to the Royal Enclosure is limited, especially for first timers. Fortunately, you will be able to view the the arrival of the monarch in a horse drawn carriage with a full royal procession at the start of the day. Another high profile equestrian event is the St Regis International Polo Cup, which takes place in May at Cowdray Park.

Wimbledon, one of the world's top tennis tournaments, takes place in London from last week of June, through to the first half of July. If you are a golfing enthusiast, do not miss the British Open, scheduled for July at Royal Troon in South Ayrshire, Scotland. The event, which has been played since 1860, is the world's oldest golf tournament. A highlight in motorcycle racing is the Manx Grand Prix, which usually takes place in August or September and serves as a great testing ground for future talent. The British Grand Prix takes place at Silverstone in Northamptonshire. A sporting event that occupies a special

LEEDS TRAVEL GUIDE

place in popular culture is the annual boat race that usually takes place in April between the university teams of Oxford and Cambridge. The tradition goes back to 1829 and draws large numbers of spectators to watch from the banks of the Thames. The FA Cup final, which is played at Wembley Stadium in May, is a must for soccer fans. As a sports event, the London Marathon is over 100 years old and draws entries from around the world to claim its prize money of a million pounds. Keen athletes will only have a brief window period of less than a week to submit their entries. Selection is by random ballot. The 42km race takes place in April.

Cultural

If you want to brush shoulders with some of your favourite authors or get the chance to pitch to a British publisher or agent, you dare not miss the London Book Fair. The event takes place in April and includes talks, panel discussions and exhibitions by a large and diverse selection of publishing role players. The London Art Fair happens in January and features discussions, tours and performances. For comic geeks there are several annual events in the UK to look forward to. The CAPTION comic convention in Oxford, which goes back to the early 1990s, is a must if you want to show your support to Britain's small presses. There is a Scottish Comic Con that takes place in the Edinburgh International Conference Center in April and a Welsh Comic Con, also in April, at Wrexham. The MCM London Comic Con happens over the last weekends of May and October, and covers anime, manga, cosplay, gaming and science fiction in general. The UK's calendar of film festivals clearly shows its cultural diversity. The oldest events are the London Film Festival (October) and the Leeds Film Festival (November). There are also large events in Manchester and Cambridge. The high-profile Encounters festival for shorts and animated films takes place each September in Bristol.

History fans can immerse themselves in the thrills and delights of the Glastonbury Medieval Fayre, which takes place in April and includes stalls, jousting and minstrels. The Tewkesbury Medieval Festival takes place in summer and its key event is the re-enactment of the Battle of Tewkesbury.

Edinburgh has an annual International Film Festival that takes place in June. The city also hosts a broader cultural festival that takes place in August. The Edinburgh International Festival is a three week event that features a packed programme of music, theatre, dance and opera, as well as talks and workshops. The Royal Highland show takes place in June and features agricultural events as well as show jumping. If you want to experience the massing of Scottish pipers, one good opportunity is the Braemar Gathering, an event that takes place on the first Saturday in September and is usually attended by the Royal family. Its roots go back 900 years. Over the spring and summer seasons, you can attend numerous Highland Games, which feature Scottish piping, as well as traditional sports such as hammer throw and tug of war. For Scottish folk dancing, attend the Cowal Highland Gathering, which takes place towards the end of August.

Websites of Interest

http://www.visitbritain.com
http://www.myguidebritain.com/
http://wikitravel.org/en/United_Kingdom
http://www.english-heritage.org.uk/
http://www.celticcastles.com/
http://www.tourist-information-uk.com/

Travel Apps

If you are planning to use public transport around the UK, get Journey Pro to help make the best connections.
https://itunes.apple.com/gb/app/journey-pro-london-uk-by-navitime/id388628933

LEEDS TRAVEL GUIDE

The Around Me app will help you to orient, if you are looking for the nearest ATM, gas station or other convenience services. http://www.aroundmeapp.com/

If you are worried about missing out on a must-see attraction in a particular area, use the National Trust's app to check out the UK's natural and historical treasures.

http://www.nationaltrust.org.uk/features/app-privacy-policy

Printed in Great Britain
by Amazon